Noddy Goes Shopping

Sticker Storybook

HarperCollins *Children's Books*

Noddy sticker storybook

This new series of *Noddy sticker storybooks* has been developed by an educational expert, using favourite Noddy stories. Key words in the story are presented as pictures, making the story text more appealing and less challenging to beginner readers.

Learning to read can be a daunting task. Working through the book together with your child can make reading fun and help develop word recognition skills.

thought hard. "A small black stone, to make my eyes feel heavy."

"Right," said Noddy. "A small black stone."

"And a few little white balls of cotton wool to use as ear plugs. Oh, yes, and a 🔦, to remind me of the calming moonlight."

Big Ears   torch

How to use the book

- Choose a quiet time to enjoy this book with your child, away from other distractions.

- Read the story aloud, making sure that your child understands what is happening. Talk about the meaning of any unfamiliar words.

- Encourage your child to 'read' each picture word out loud at the appropriate time in the story.

- After reading each page, ask your child to find the matching stickers from the pages in the middle of the book.

- Help your child to put each sticker in the right place on the bottom of the page.

- Say the picture words aloud together.

- Don't forget to praise your child for helping you to read the story!

- Encourage them to retell the story in their own words, using the pictures to remind them what has happened.

It was a peaceful morning in  when
Noddy's  hurtled through the streets.
PARP! PARP! "We made it!" gasped Mrs Skittle as
the car screeched to a halt at the  .
"Now, Noddy," she said.
"How much do I owe you?"

 Toy Town  car  station

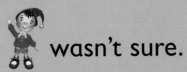 wasn't sure.

"Um, did I say two children count as one grown up, or…"

"Noddy!" cried ."I'm in a hurry. Here! Keep the change." And she dropped a heap of 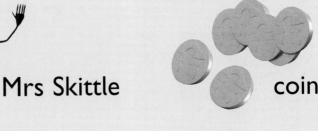 into his hand.

"Oh!" cried Noddy. "What a lot of money!"

 Noddy   Mrs Skittle   coins

Noddy jumped into his car and zoomed across town to Big-Ears'  .

"Hello, Big-Ears!" cried Noddy, running up the  . "I've just earned loads of money. We could go out and spend it on… oh!" He stopped in surprise.

 Toadstool House

 stairs

Big-Ears was still in  !

"Big-Ears! It's the middle of the morning and you're still asleep!" said  .

"I wish I was asleep," Big-Ears yawned, loudly. "That's the problem. I just can't seem to get to sleep at all."

 Bed

 Noddy

"Then why don't you go to bed early?" suggested Noddy.

"I can't get to sleep!" said  crossly.

"If I weren't so tired, I'd go into town to buy the things I need to make a sleeping charm."

"I'll go for you!" offered Noddy.

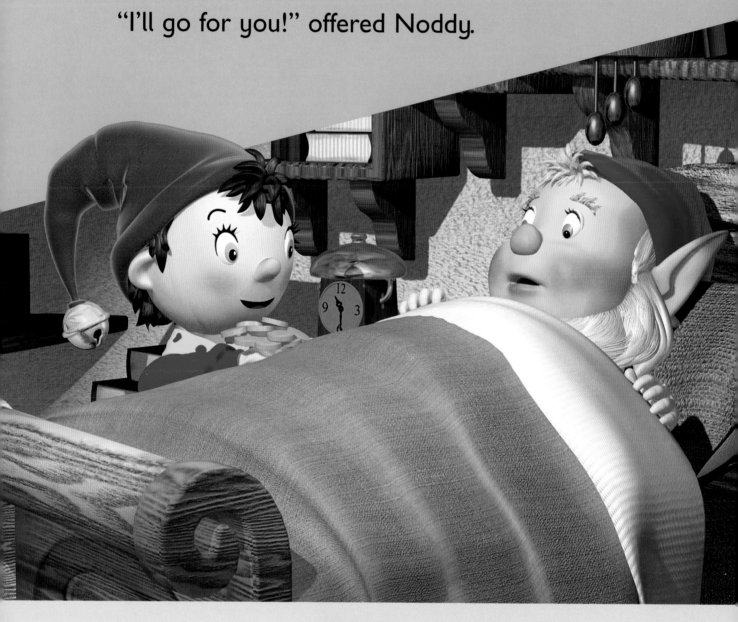

Big-Ears

"That's very kind," said Big-Ears. "Now, listen: I'll need a small cloth  to hold everything."
"A small cloth bag," repeated Noddy. "Got it."
"A bunch of night-blooming  to make me feel sleepy."
"OK," said Noddy. "What else?"

bag   flowers

 thought hard. "A small black stone, to make my eyes feel heavy."

"Right," said Noddy. "A small black stone."

"And a few little white balls of cotton wool to use as ear plugs. Oh, yes, and a  , to remind me of the calming moonlight."

Big-Ears   torch

"You must remember all the things," said Big-Ears. "If you forget just one of them, the charm won't work."

"Don't worry, Big-Ears!" said .

Big-Ears yawned. "And I also need a toy ," he said. "It'll get me snoring."

 Noddy   saw

"That's six things to remember," said Noddy, as he headed for the . "I won't forget any of them!"

Big-Ears checked the time on the .

"Noddy should be back in about half an hour."

And he settled back to wait.

door   clock

One hour and forty-five minutes later, Noddy had still not come back.

"Where on earth is Noddy?" yawned  .

"He should be back by now."

Big-Ears

The  ticked away.

But still Noddy did not come back. Big-Ears grew more and more worried.

Just then, he heard the front  open, and the sound of eager footsteps coming up the  .

clock

door

stairs

"I'm back!" cried Noddy, bursting into the room.

"What took you so long?" asked Big-Ears.

"Sorry," said Noddy, dumping a large  on the floor. "It just took a while to get all six things."

box

"Here's the cloth bag," said Noddy, pulling a large  out of the box. peered into it.

"I can't see any little bag. Are you sure it's in here?"

sack

Big-Ears

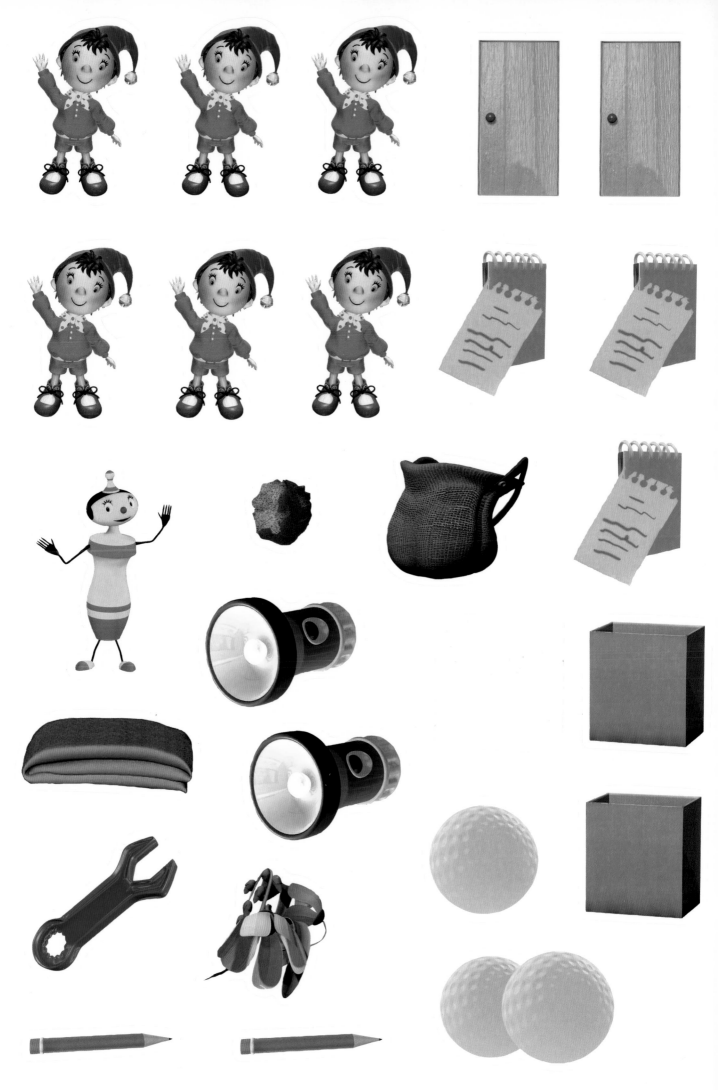

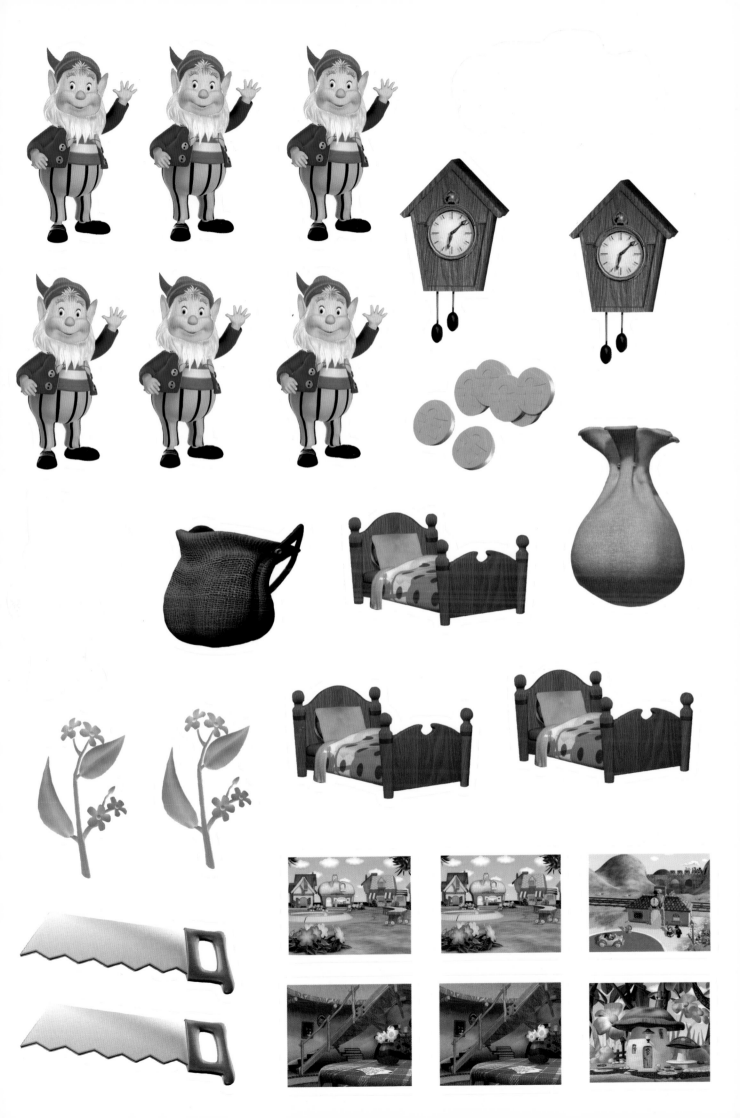

"It's not in the sack," laughed Noddy.

"It **is** the sack!"

"Noddy," groaned Big-Ears,

"I said a small ."

"Oops!" said 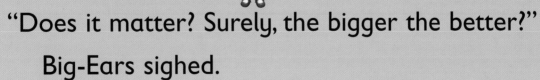.

"Does it matter? Surely, the bigger the better?"

Big-Ears sighed.

bag

Noddy

"What about the ear plugs?" asked Big-Ears.

Noddy handed Big-Ears some hard white balls.

"Oh, no! Not  !" wailed Big-Ears.

I said cotton wool balls."

Noddy shrugged. "All I could remember was white balls. Sorry!"

golf balls

 shook his head. "Well, Noddy… did you remember the small black stone?"

Noddy pulled a big, grey rock out of the  .

"Honestly, Noddy," frowned Big-Ears.

"I said a small black stone. This is big and grey!"

Big-Ears 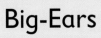 box

"Oh, dear. I forgot about the size," said Noddy.
"But I didn't forget the colour!"

He pulled out a black  and started
scribbling on the .

"Have you remembered anything properly?"
moaned Big-Ears.

Noddy put his hand back into the box.

pencil rock

"What is that for?" asked , crossly.

"A car headlight for your moonlight, silly!" said Noddy. "Now you don't remember!"

"No, no, no, no, no!" cried Big-Ears.

"I said a , not a headlight."

"Won't a headlight do?" asked Noddy.

 Big-Ears

torch

"Well, at least I remembered the tool to make you snore!" said Noddy.

Big-Ears couldn't believe Noddy had been so silly. "I said , Noddy. Not ."

"Oh dear!" said Noddy. "But look, you could try this…" And he put the spanner on his nose.

saw   spanner

Big-Ears pulled the spanner off Noddy's nose.

"I expect you've muddled up the  as well," sighed Big-Ears.

Noddy put his hand into the box and pulled out a bunch of dead .

"Wrong!" groaned Big-Ears. "Just like everything else!"

 flowers

 weeds

"Noddy," Big-Ears said sadly, "you didn't remember
one single thing."

"I'm really sorry, Big-Ears," said .
"I just don't have a very good memory."

Big-Ears smiled. "No, you don't!"

"I tried my best, Big-Ears, truly I did," sighed Noddy.

Noddy

"I know," said Big-Ears, kindly, "but if you need to remember something, write it down."

"What a good idea!" whooped Noddy, happily.

Big-Ears picked up a  and quickly wrote out a shopping  .

 pencil  list

"Thanks," said Noddy. "Now I'll remember everything!" And he picked up the  and rushed downstairs.

Seconds later, he was back.

"Err… I forgot the , Big-Ears," he said as he grabbed it.

box

list

Big-Ears grinned as he shuffled back to  .

"That boy… Oops!" Big-Ears' foot slipped
on a  .

BOING! He hit the bed and then bounced up to
the ceiling. THWACK! Down he came with a
mighty THUD! Big-Ears was out cold!

Bed   golf ball

A little while later,  came back.

"I managed to get everything on the !"
he called. "Now you can get some sleep,
Big-Ears. … oh!"

He stopped, staring in astonishment.

Noddy   list

"Zzzz-zzzz-zzzz." Big-Ears was fast asleep, snoring loudly. He looked very comfortable. Noddy crept over to the  . "Maybe you didn't need the sleeping charm after all," he whispered.

Bed

"Good night!" said Noddy, and he pulled the  gently over  and tiptoed out. "Zzzzzzzzzzzzz…"

blanket

Big-Ears

This edition first published by HarperCollins *Children's Books* in 2008.
HarperCollins *Children's Books* is a division of HarperCollins Publishers Ltd, 77-85 Fulham Palace Rd,
Hammersmith, London, W6 8JB.

10 9 8 7 6 5 4 3 2 1

ISBN: 0-00-727363-0
ISBN-13: 978-0-00-727363-8
Printed and bound in China
www.Noddy.com
A CIP catalogue for this title is available from the British Library.

The HarperCollins *Children's Books* website is:
www.harpercollinschildrensbooks.co.uk

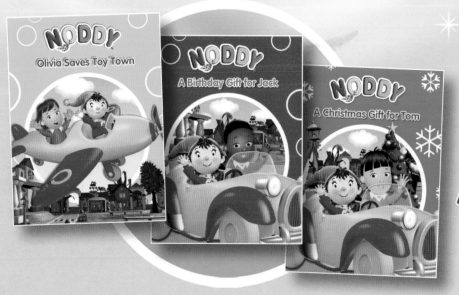